To Sanity And Back
Back
A Jimbo's Tale

To Cindy
Sanity is overrated
Enjoy the book
I will miss you
love Jim
SST

D1092484

Jim Fairhurst

DEDICATION

I dedicate this book to all my family and friends, past, current, and future. Especially to my grandchild who is currently under construction. May he/she be healthy, wealthy, and wise, but above all happy.

Contents

4

Disclaimer / Introduction

I started writing poetry to my girlfriend who later became my wife. For many years she was the only audience of my poems, after all she was the intended recipient of them all. Later the recipient list grew, I would write the odd poem to family, mum, dad, daughter, etc. For the most part I would write them for special occasions like birthdays or anniversaries, but occasionally other significant events would happen. Work events or Karate events would inspire me to write something.

Then in 2020 I was issued a challenge to do something for 30 days during our first month of lock-down during the Covid-19 crisis. I selected to write a poem every day for the entire month. I must say I had a great time. So in 2021 I decided to try this challenge again. Both years and many of my other poems are included in this book.

Here's a glimpse into my soul, a view beyond the mask,
To wade through all the crazy, and in the genius bask.

My thoughts are put in stanzas, many of which rhyme,
Read them all and you'll understand if you give it time.

Many are light hearted, they're just a little humour,
Others are a bit more dark, they're like a little tumor.

Some may be political, and some may be quite crude,
Some are made up nonsense and some are downright lewd.

So if my poems offend you please take my advice,
Go take your sensitive body parts and stick them in a vice.

April 2020 30 Day (Poem-a-day) Challenge

During my 2020 Month of Poems challenge I sent my work colleagues a poem every day. Towards the end of the month I did write a couple each day, as I had requested the recipients to share some topics they would like me to write about. The next 34 poems are the poems I sent to my colleagues. However I did write a few extras that were not appropriate to send at the time. I have included the extra poems in their own section towards the back of the book.

April 1st 2020

Day one, challenge accepted, A poem every day.
This won't be very easy, But I'll try it anyway.

I will write them with the doggies, I will write them with a view.
I will write them at my PC, I will write them on the loo.

They may be about the virus, Or other scary stuff.
I have a stack of topics, I'm sure there'll be enough.

If you're easily offended, Step away from this 'ere book.
Do not flip the pages, And do not take a look!

My poems can be sassy, Sometimes they're downright crude.
Their intent is always harmless, So stop being such a prude.

April 2nd 2020

The second day, this aint so bad, it's really kinda neat,
I hope this month-long journey through my brain is quite a treat.

I'm going to share my good times, I'll also share my gripes,
But I'll make sure that I clean them first with disinfectant wipes.

Day one was kinda normal, except I ate more snacks,
Sending my newsletter, and filing income tax.

Day two's not so good though, we have some server probs,
It looks like someone has been in, playing with the knobs.

I really must be going cos I have a class to do,
I shall say bye-bye for now, that's the end of number two.

April 3rd 2020

I'm sitting here at my PC, just working through my emails,
I see one from the server that shows the backup fails.

So I'm logging in remotely to see what's going on,
Another friendly screw-up from our network guy called John.

No backups of our data, no backups of our apps,
Let's hope there's no more problems with all these ancient scraps.

At least our email's working, thank god for our G Suite,
That's one tech choice that we made right, cos Google can't be beat.

I'm sure that we can fix it, just another normal day,
I'm just thankful that it's Friday, tomorrow I can play.

April 4th 2020

Oh Amazon, oh Amazon, the store we get to browse,
It sells appliances, and clothing, groceries and ploughs.

A week or so for shipping, it's hardly ever late,
What else have we to do, but sit in our house and wait.

With a smile upon the package, unless it's upside down,
It saves us from that scary trip to shops that are in town.

You add stuff to your wishlist, you add it to your cart,
It's never ever closed, and it's cleaner than Walmart.

Oh Amazon, oh Amazon, the store that's in the cloud,
I wore the clothes, I ate the food, and with the plough I ploughed.

Support your favorite charity by going to smile.amazon.com.

April 5th 2020

Sunday morning paddle, the best time of the week,
It's an oasis of some good times in a future that is bleak.

Sunday brunch is cancelled, I really miss that grub,
But most of all I miss my buds in the breakfast club.

The ocean's nice and clear, the water's not too rough,
The paddle out was easy, the paddle back's a little tough.

I forgot to start my watch again, to track my paddle route,
I'm sure we did six miles, of that I have no doubt.

No whale today or dolphin, no manta and no shark,
I guess they're social distancing, just like the rest of Clark[1].

---

[1] Clark is the company I was working for at the time.

April 6th 2020

Another conference call, this one's at five a.m.
The art of watching paint dry, this one will be a gem.

I'm sitting in my P.J.s, a meeting to attend.
I'll keep my camera covered, cos I don't want to offend.

I'm waiting for the call to start, I'm the only one that's here.
Nobody else has joined yet, I'm off to get a beer.

The first one in's a caller who can not find the mute,
Their kids are in the background practising their flute.

The next arrives with camera just pointing up their nose,
A few more join, the meeting starts, and someone's desktop shows.

We talk about the weather, we talk about the news,
We talk about our doggies, I'm off to get more booze.

April 7th 2020

Some days are filled with beauty, some are filled with pain.
Some days are gorgeous sunshine, some are constant rain.

So when you're feeling grumpy, and your life's a little sad.
Just think about tomorrow, it could be twice as bad.

The future's not a sure thing, it's never guaranteed.
Don't wish away the present, driving through life at top speed.

Take your time and smell the roses, or whatever flower you chose,
Just don't smell self-raising, the powder gets up your nose.

April 8th 2020

A pleasant evening paddle, a rainbow in the sky,
A shaka in the distance, from a paddler passing by.

Spinners on the port side, playing in the waves,
Pretty rock formations inside the lava caves.

Turtles on the nearby rocks sleeping in the sun,
More spinners right behind us, having lots of fun.

Schools of tiny fishes, in the clear blue sea,
Another awesome paddle, just my other half and me.

We wash the boat and store it, then head back to our home,
Then I sit down and I start to write, another little poem.

April 9th 2020

There is a dog named Chewie, to us he's kinda new,
When we take him on a walk he fills 3 bags with poo.

He was old when we first got him, and his breath was pretty rank,
He's such a chunky monkey, mommy's paddleboard just sank.

He sometimes gets in my way, he sometimes makes me curse,
He's such a little stinker, I'm not sure which end smells worse.

Manini kinda likes him, but she sometimes gets real jealous,
She can play a little too rough, sometimes she's over zealous.

He's no longer being fostered, he no longer has to roam,
He's now in our ohana, he's found himself a home.

April 10th 2020

Working at my home desk, a pillow on my knee.
Sat upon the pillow, is my puppy Manini.

Chewie's in the other room, sitting with my spouse.
Oreo's in the kitchen, she's queen of the whole house.

Barry's on his rounds, sweeping up the floor.
We've rolled up the front door mat, so he can't go out the door.

Barry is the Robot vac, the wife had named it that.
Oreo's the granddaughter, but she really is a cat.

We haven't named the fridge yet, but I'm sure we'll do it soon.
I'm leaning towards Elsa, but she wants to be called June.

April 11th 2020

If I could choose to come back as any kind of beast,
I'd come back as a dolphin, on fishes I would feast.

I'd have fun in the ocean, I wouldn't have to work,
I'd knock off all the surfers, cos I would be a jerk.

I'd hang with other dolphins, cos they would be like me,
I would swim quite close to shore, I would swim far out to sea.

If I could choose how I would come back, you all know what I wish,
I would be a dolphin, so long and thanks for all the fish.

April 12th 2020

Happy Easter Sunday, a day to celebrate,
Chocolate eggs and bunnies, a day to get up late.

I'm going on my hunt now, for little Easter eggs,
I hope the hunt's not too long, too far for my small legs.

I will search inside the bedroom, I will search inside the loo,
I will search within the dining room, I will search the kitchen too.

Oh wow I think I found them, hiding in plain sight,
They're in the fridge in an egg box colored all in white.

I wonder what's inside them, chocolate, toys and more,
I open up my treasures, now I have egg yoke on the floor.

April 13th 2020

I'm only on day thirteen, I'm already cooking meth.
The coffee's just not strong enough and it's playing hell with my fresh breath.

My brain is going wonky, I may be going mad.
The gecko's talking to me, he says his name is Brad.

My keyboard smells of purple, and my mouse, it sounds like green.
My slippahs went out for a walk, since then they've not been seen.

The earwigs are escaping from the holes inside my head,
The centipedes are curled up on the pillows in my bed.

My wrist is now my toothbrush, it's buzzing really loud,
My head is falling upwards, up through a fluffy cloud.

I'm not sure if I'm dreaming but it's time for me to wake,
Cos I am getting hungry, it's time for my pancake.

April 14th 2020

There was a muggle agent, computers were their bane,
The technology confused them and drove them quite insane.

Should they go with Windows, should they go with Mac?
Should they box the thing back up and send the darn thing back?

Where the heck's the on switch, how do they get connected?
Oops they made a bad mistake, now how is that corrected?

They better send a help ticket, to get the help they need,
So how do they submit it, the instructions they should read.

They open up their browser and go to the bookmark,
A special one created, just for those that work at Clark.

They hit the submit button after filling all the fields,
Then they sit there waiting to see what that action yields.

Five minutes have gone by, why don't the guys respond?
Why haven't those tech guys waved their magic wand?

The Tech guys are quite busy, both stuck in their own homes,
One is helping agents, one is writing poems.

April 15th 2020

I'm halfway through this challenge, so far it's been quite easy,
I hope I've entertained you and not been far too cheesy.

When this challenge is all over, and 30 poems I have penned,
I will stick them all into a book, that's what I intend.

I have so many others I've written over time,
I am quite determined that every one will rhyme.

Of all the many poems that I wrote throughout the years,
Most are filled with laughter, some are filled with tears.

Many written for my wife, not for anyone to view,
All the others are about my life, sounds odd, but it is true.

April 16th 2020

We drove to get the test done and they hold up a sign,
They ask a bunch of questions, so far it's going fine.

They wander back into the tent, what are they going to do?
They put on all their armor so they don't get sick too,

They come back out protected with gloves and mask and shield,
In their hand the testing kit that they're about to wield.

And then they take a sample, and this is how it goes,
They take a foot long cotton swab and stuff it up your nose.

They wiggle it and spin it and pull it out again,
That cotton swab is long enough to take samples of your brain.

Then they let you know that a whole week you must wait,
And till the test comes in, we must self isolate.

April 17th 2020

Once I ate a live worm, it was really kinda gritty,
Now it's time to honor that worm and write a little ditty.

It was minding its own business just wriggling in the dirt,
Then I bent down and I picked it up and wiped it on my shirt.

I put it in my mouth and bite down on the guy,
It's at this point I ask myself oh why, oh God, oh why?

I may have cleaned the outside, but the inside's full of grit,
And now my teeth were crunching on a mouthful of worm $hit.

At the time I felt real sorry, but not for it for me,
Cos that disgusting little action only got me 50p.

April 18th 2020

Today's a day to celebrate, today's a day to cheer,
Because we got the results back and it says all clear.

Today's a day to smile, today we can go out,
But only for essential things with a mask over our snout.

We might go out to Walmart, and maybe Target too,
But MickyD's is closed so what are we to do?

Where will we get our soda, where will we sit and chat?
I guess we'll go back home again and sit with grumpy cat.

I'm going out to paddle, and get back on my boat,
I hope that with the weight I've gained, I still can stay afloat.

April 19th 2020

About 9 million species are living on this globe,
One is causing chaos, and it aint that small microbe.

No the one that I'm referring, is not a little germ,
It's bigger than a virus, it's bigger than a worm.

It is a vicious mammal, sat on top of the food chain,
It's supposed to be quite clever, with quite a lot of brain.

It squanders all the resources the planet has to give,
It thinks just cos it's smartest, it has more right to live.

It makes me sad to think of all the wildlife they kill,
The Earth does keep a tally, and they're racking up a bill.

The Earth will get it's vengeance, cos it really is quite riled,
These creatures are called humans, they deserve to be exiled.

April 20th 2020

I'm back out on the ocean, virtual racing I can do,
As long as there's no others on the water with me too.

I paddle out the harbour, I stop, adjust my crotch,
Get ready for 6 miles and then I set my watch.

My watch connects to satellites and buzzes every mile,
So each time that it buzzes, I crack a little smile.

When it get to three miles, it's time to turn around,
Then it's only three more and I'm back on solid ground.

I stop the watch at six to measure my race time,
Then on my drive back home, I start this little rhyme.

April 21st 2020

I better put the coffee on, I'm going to need a mug.
Oh wait I've got a meeting, I'd better make a jug.

A stimulant is needed when I've meetings to attend,
It doesn't matter who it's with, coworker or a friend.

They'd dummify the smartest, they'd moronize the great,
After sitting in a meeting my brain is second rate.

Not that the meetings bore me, sometimes they entertain,
But sometimes I come out of them with a slightly smaller brain.

My IQ was amazing, a genius it's said,
But now I might as well have rocks inside my head.

April 22nd 2020

Looking back to days of old, before this global crisis,
Where we could see our enemy, like Hezbollah or Isis.

Our news was full of minor stuff like impeachment or mass shootings,
Or Middle eastern riots and the subsequent shop lootings.

The stocks were up, unemployment low, the headlines often read,
Not, another hundred thousand from Corona are now dead.

So hunker down with a box of chocs, and your whiskey flask,
And if you should need to go outside, wear your freaking mask!

April 23rd 2020

I'm on my OC1 again for another 6 mile run,
I see the ocean's bumpy, alright this should be fun.

I have my headphones in, so I can't hear what you're saying,
The surf is getting feisty and the DollyRots are playing.

I must be going up hill, this paddle's really hard,
Twenty five strokes later and I've barely moved a yard.

The journey back should be a breeze if this way is so tough,
But by the time I turn around I'm running out of puff.

I catch a bump or two, but nothing really lasting,
So I switch my songs to more upbeat and get that sucker blasting.

I finish up the six, but I'm really kinda bushed,
I didn't beat my record, but I know myself I pushed.

April 24th 2020

Oh coffee mug I worship thee, you're my saviour in the morning,
Without you I would wander lost, and there'd be no amber warning.

To struggle forth without coffee, would be an evil sin,
For when I've had my coffee, the day I'm sure to win.

It revives me from my slumber, my focus it doth hones,
It wakes my weary body, it wakes my weary bones.

I sip thee down to quench my need, for energy and vigor,
For without coffee by my side, the day would seem much bigger.

So praises go to caffeine and the bean it comes inside.
Let coffee be my power source, let coffee be my guide.

April 25th 2020

I may be running out of topics on which to write my composition
I may need some assistance with the rest.

If you want to send a topic to help me with my mission
I'm sure the last few ones will be my best.

So send me a quick email with a subject of a ditty,
And I will do my best to make it rhyme.

The subject can be anything, serious or witty,
But hurry up I'm running out of time.

April 26th 2020

Response for Jennifer Tanaka - Your Wedding Day

September 3rd in eighty eight was the second best day of my life,
Why was that day special, it was the day that I married my wife.

She looked so pretty in her dress, as she walked down the aisle,
I stood there gazing back at her, all I could do was smile.

I wore top hat and tails, she wore a wedding dress,
The service went quite smoothly, but the photos were a mess.

We held our top hats upside down, just like a mixing bowl,
And there's a photo of the bride, like she's standing in a hole.

The vicar who did the service, was fairly odd to look at,
My brother-in-law brought Wally, Wally was his pet rat.

The reception was in the village hall, round the corner from the church,
If you want to see a picture just do a google search.

But this should be your best day I hear many of you warn,
Nope, the best day of my life, was when my daughter was born.

Response for Irina Koroleva - Internet Fraud

Be careful what you open, when you check your email
For it can cause a problem, your computer, it can fail.

Some email senders can't be trusted, some are not legit,
They could be spoofing, phishing or just plain full of shit.

Be cautious when conversing with people on the net,
They may not be legitimate, a phony you might get.

Don't click links willy nilly, take time to analyze,
Some links are built to deceive, they can be filled with lies.

Before you hit the reply, please verify the sender,
A help ticket you'll be sending and calling out the mender.

April 27th 2020

Response for Janet Wells Brown - The removal of your tonsils in a most unusual way

When I was growing up, in mischief I would get,
I'd knock on doors and run away, or eat an earthworm for a bet.

But I had turned my mom grey, when I was very young,
Before my teenage mischief, before worms on my tongue.

I was just a toddler when I played with my moms Hoover,
Blowing down the vacuum pipe like a shaker and a groover.

Then I slipped and fell, and that pipe went down my throat,
I sliced out my own tonsils, in my stomach they did float.

You may think I was naughty or maybe just a fool,
But I conducted surgery before I'd started school.

Response for Gae Callaway - The good-ole-days

When we say "the good ole days" what really do we mean?
Warped memories from our history that only we have seen.

Was it really all that good, or is it all just an illusion?
Is the present all that bad, or is that just our conclusion?

The bad guy-good guy ratio is no worse now than the past,
It's just that news can now travel across the globe so fast.

April 28th 2020

Response for Cyndi Dyal - About food

When I was growing up, my favorite things to eat,
Were candies and ice cream, bags of snacks, and meat.

The bags of snacks were mostly what I had at lunch,
Salt and vinegar crisps or maybe Monster Munch.

Cheese and Branston Pickle was my favorite kind of sarney,
When the weather got too cold, a bowl of chilli con carne.

For tea I might have Pukka Pie from the local chippy,
And if we heard the ice cream man I'd get a Mr Whippy.

Candies were my favorite, chocolate, fudge, or toffee,
I guess that's why I need to have many sugars in my coffee.

My best dessert was custard, a powder made by Birds,
A creamy, powdery, sweet dessert for which there are no words.

An Extra Poem for April 28th 2020

Response for Nobody

We've just run out of toilet roll, and wipes are running low,
I ate some spicy chili, now I really need to go.

I guess I will use nature, It's better than my sleeves,
I have some giant hogweed, I have some nettle leaves.

How 'bout some poison ivy, or maybe bougainvilleas,
My botty's squeaky clean now, but hell, I am in tears.

April 29th 2020 A

Sometimes a common enemy is what us humans need,
To pull us all together, to make the people heed.

If we don't work together, we're doomed to fall apart,
We need to stop being selfish, when will the kindness start?

United we may have a chance, divided is a curse,
If us humans stay the same, we're gonna need a bigger hearse.

At this time of crisis, we really must unite,
It's only when we're unified, this virus we can fight.

We should work together, join forces and agree,
Collaborate, conspire, that's all of you and me.

Team-up, and cooperate, then this bug we'll slay,
If we all stand together, but stand six feet away.

April 29th 2020 B

This challenge was a lot of fun, it really was a blast,
30 days was not too hard, the days went by so fast.

I wrote 40 poems in one month, that's a few more than I mailed,
If the Feds were listening in they may well get me jailed.

The missing ones were cruel, the missing ones were mean,
It may be best for these missing ones to hide away unseen.

Unless you need to know, unless you're really curious,
But I don't want to offend you, I don't want to make you furious.

There are three taboo subjects, to discuss it's not polite,
Unless you want to argue, or end up in a fight.

Do not discuss religion, discussing sex is banned,
Don't discuss politics, or you may just end up canned.

So the last few will stay hidden, unless you're sure they won't offend,
In which case just DM me and to just you I will send.

April 30th 2020

I am a first time buyer, I want to buy a home,
I no longer want to rent, I no longer want to roam.

It needs to have one bedroom, for me to lay my head,
It needs to have a second one, for a guest to have a bed,

It needs to have a third, somewhere to throw my coat,
It should also have a study, so I can work remote.

It needs to have two bathrooms, and each to have two sinks,
The second one's for me to use, when the first one stinks.

One bathroom needs to be quite big, it needs a walk-in shower,
I also want some solar panels so I can save on power

It needs to have a gym, so I can stay in shape,
It needs to have a gameroom, so I can just escape.

The kitchen should be massive, I love to entertain,
The carpets should be treated, I don't want them to stain.

It need some propane tanks so I can do some baking,
I don't want any trees, cos I really don't like raking.

It needs a garden shed, so I can store my tools,
A big one for my mower, my ride-on really rules.

It needs to have an ocean view, I also need a mountain,
It needs to have a swimming pool, with a hot tub and a fountain.

It needs a quiet neighborhood, I don't want too much noise.
It must have a large back yard, to fit my seven boys.

It must be free from insects, and from coqui frogs,
It must be near the walking trails so I can walk the dogs.

It must be near the beach, so I can go and surf,
And automatic sprinklers underneath my turf.

It needs to have a garage, that fits my trucks and bikes,
It needs to be near nature, so I can go on hikes.

It's gotta be near Costco, and also quite near school,
But not on a school bus route, that would be uncool.

My driveway needs a gate I can open from my truck,
That might keep the riff raff out, it might with any luck.

I dont wanna pay commission you've gotta do it free,
You should feel it's an honor, to help someone like me.

April 2021 30 Day (Poem-a-day) Challenge Part II

The following 30 poems were sent out to work colleagues for the April 2021 Month of Poems challenge. Any extra poems that I wrote during this month but didn't send out are placed later in the book.

April 1st 2021

Twas a year ago a challenge I started,
When a poem a day I wrote, spoke, or farted.

Some turned out good, some turned out shite,
So I start some more, I hope they're alright.

These poems I write are stories of me,
A view from my eyes, stuff that I see.

But also the feelings and thoughts from inside,
So hold on to something, this could be a ride.

I have brand new topics, I have old ones too,
I've written down subjects, I've written a few.

I hope you will like them, and they don't annoy,
So go grab a cuppa, sit back, and enjoy.

If you know someone crazy, a little insane,
They too are welcome to journey my brain.

Just send them a link to my signup list,
But only the crazy, of this I insist.

https://sites.google.com/view/jimsemailsignup/

April 2nd 2021

I'm going to be a grandpa, how awesome will it be?
To have a mini Whitney Jade, or pocket sized C3.

They just sent us the news, it's gonna be a boy,
But whatever it is going to be, it's gonna be a joy.

He's sure to be quite dapper, he's sure to be quite cute,
And when he eats his beans up, I'm pretty sure he'll toot.

He's sure to be quite tall, if he takes after his dad,
If he takes after his grandpa, he'll be a porkie lad.

He'll be quite a trend setter, with style, panache, and flair.
A wardrobe full of romper suits, and aloha wear,

A bunch of tiny diapers, for a tiny little bum,
A superhero baby for a super dad and mum.

April 3rd 2021

I'm sitting out here with my pups on my lap,
Drinking some coffee and reading some crap.

I look at the ground and notice a slug,
And wonder what life must be like as a bug.

Worried that birds will come bite off your head,
Crawling on chemicals that make you dead.

Living a life that's only two years,
Having 4 noses, but not any ears.

One tiny blow hole and three thousand teeth,
Only one foot, and slime underneath.

Leaving a trail that squirms all around,
That is what life's like down here on the ground.

April 4th 2021

I'm a rona virus, I'm floating through the air,
I may land on a table, I may land on a chair.

I'm the rona virus, I'm looking for a ride,
I was coughed out from my last host, before the fella died.

I am the rona virus, i'm harmless people say,
I'll jump into your system and change your DNA.

I'm the rona virus, I'm sure we'll have some fun
Well I know that I sure will, but you, I think you're done.

I'm the rona virus, and you don't look so great,
You better see a doctor before it is too late.

I'm the rona virus, and my ride is at its end,
So pass me on to someone else, I'll see you later, friend.

April 5th 2021

Many years ago when I was just a nipper,
If I behaved real badly I wouldn't get the slipper.

I'd get the wooden spoon, but not a normal one,
This one was freaking massive, and really wasn't fun.

She'd grab it from the wall, I'd run away in fear,
She'd chase me round the house, and smack me on the rear.

But now that wooden spoon has many chips and dents,
So when she grabs it off the wall, I'd run, that's my 2 cents.

When I was feeling poorly, or had a painful tum,
I'd get the day off school and stay home with my mum.

Then the second after school starts, I'd be well enough to play,
Too late to go to school though, I'd stay at home all day.

The Lego bricks are scattered across the front room floor,
With the bricks I'd build my weapons, so I'd be ready for the war.

Rubber bands and Lego, a working crossbow makes,
Until mum's china ornament it accidentally breaks.

Then out comes that old spoon again and I begin to run,
I should not have made a crossbow, I should have made a gun.

April 6th 2021

A chill in the morning, no moon in the sky,
I go for a paddle, but I wonder why.
It's too dark to see where the heck I am going
It's too cold for me, it feels like it's snowing.

I look at the temperature gauge in the Jeep,
And hope that the number, upwards will creep.
Just one degree higher and I will be fine,
Cos I am a weaner and cold makes me whine.

Then over the mountain I see signs of our star,
The warmth of the light that's travelled so far.
The temp has gone up by just one degree,
But that is enough to paddle for me.

It went up from twenty to twenty one C,
Twenty's too cold I'm sure you'll agree.
But twenty one celsius is so much better,
Anything less and I'm wearing a sweater.

I head to the harbor and jump in the canoe,
Just 5 or 6 miles is what we will do.
Then head into work, to help all the muggles,
With an evening at home for some puppy dog snuggles.

April 7th 2021

Grandad, or Grandpa, or Gramps, or Pappy
I wonder the name that he will call me.

Grandma or Nanny or Gran or Tutu
I wonder the name that he will call you

For under construction a grandson there be
I can't wait to see him, and him to see me.

A small precious life, a bundle of joy
In my baby girl grows a baby boy.

She'll make a great mum, loving and kind
And Chris a great dad, the best one could find.

Between them they'll raise him to be honest and true
They'll wipe his small butt when he's done a poo.

They'll teach him to draw or make creepy things,
Like a doll with eight eyes, and removable wings.

But whatever he does, It's gonna be great,
We're really excited, we just can not wait.

April 8th 2021

We painted the spare bedroom, we painted it bright yellow.
We did the master bedroom blue, but it's a bit more mellow.

We did the hallway loofah, it's a brownish creamish hue.
The front room's slightly darker, a little more like poo.

It's now the bathroom's turn to get a renovation.
But it's looks don't really worry me, it's just a doodoo station.

I don't spend too much time in there just gazing at it's looks.
The time I spend while I'm in there I'm reading comic books.

She wants a cruise ship shower to replace the aging tub,
It may be kinda tiny, but that's less tile to scrub.

We'll rip out the small closet and gain some extra space,
And add a nice big mirror so I can see my face.

We will change out all the flooring and replace the vanity,
But will we finish the project, before loss of sanity?

We'll have to use the spare bath while the main one's in a mess,
I know, when done, I'll like it, of that I must confess.

April 9th 2021

It's four thirty in the morning, a wet nose on my cheek,
I get up and let the dog out so she can take a leak.

I sit and eat my oatmeal, then give some to the pup,
Sure miss my Lucky Charms though, but I guess I'm now grown up.

I get dressed in my work clothes and grab my phone and keys,
I wish Cathy a good day, then give the pups a squeeze.

I drive down to the office, and i put the coffee on,
Give it 2 more hours, that pot will be all gone.

I read through all my emails and plan the day ahead,
Wishing all along I was still tucked up in bed.

A photograph to edit, an email blast to send,
A PC with a virus for me to clean and mend.

A day of helping agents with all their PC woes,
But still no darn help tickets, I guess that's how it goes.

April 10th 2021

The view from our house is a sight to behold,
A scene full of ocean that never gets old.

I know I am lucky, I appreciate life,
Me here in paradise along with my wife.

The weather is perfect, it's 80 degrees,
A smell from the flowers of plumeria trees.

The hillside is dotted with hibiscus and palms,
Just some of this island's so many charms.

The fruit trees bare plenty right in our backyard,
We can grow anything, it's really not hard.

Look up to the sky in the middle of night,
The stars in the sky are always so bright.

The people are great, they're friendly and kind,
This place we call home is a hell of a find.

There's just one more thing that I need to say,
There's no other place that I'd rather stay.

April 11th 2021

My first shot is done so I sit back and wait,
I do hope my powers won't show up too late.

I wonder just which super powers I'll get,
I will use them for good, you don't have to fret.

Will I get super smart, or become really fast?
Will my eyes or my hands shoot an energy blast?

Will I get healing powers, or have x-ray sight?
Will I control weather, or maybe just light?

Able to shrink, or stretch really long?
Read others' thoughts or get super strong?

Will I control tech, or will I control time?
What power will I get so I can stop crime?

Maybe my powers won't be quite so grand,
They may be more subtle, more modest, more bland.

My superhero name could be hipster boy
And my super power, I can wear corduroy.

April 12th 2021

Oh little tadpole can you find your way?
To find the flying saucer and share your DNA?

To make a little zygote, a little embryo,
It then becomes a fetus, with nowt to do but grow.

It's legs and feet are forming, with tiny little toes
Every day it's bigge,r everyday it grows.

It's arms and hands are forming, with digits of their own,
It starts to feel around, in it's amniotic zone.

The organs have all formed and the face is more defined
It investigates it's lodgings to see what it can find.

There's a wall upon the right side, and on the left side too,
It can't find a way out, oh what is it to do?

It punches and it kicks, it's getting cramped in there,
It wants to get it's freedom, it wants that gulp of air.

But more than anything it wants to see it's mum,
But first of all the doctor's going to smack it on the bum.

April 13th 2021

We have a homeless problem, I think we all agree,
They hang around in alleys and sleep under a tree.

They defecate in doorways, and don't pick up their trash,
They stand at intersections just begging for some cash.

Some are kinda crazy, and some are kinda feral,
If they were cats we'd round them up and make them kinda sterile.

Some are very scary, they yell, and scream and curse
Then policemen come along and tell them to disperse.

They push the shopping trolley filled up with all their junk
I don't know where they get the booze but most of them are drunk

But some of them aren't crazy, we just misunderstand
All they need is some assistance, a little helping hand.

I don't like giving handouts, putting money in their cup
I'd rather give them half my food, not handout but hand up.

April 14th 2021

It's National Dolphin Day

Dolphins are warm blooded, they all have lungs and hair,
They're very social creatures that like to play and share.

Dolphins are intelligent, more than us I think,
They don't have to go to work, or pay a pricy shrink.

They get to play and frolic out in the food filled sea,
Which of us is stupid, I think the answer's me.

Dolphins do have politics, but its not filled with greed,
It's used to help the whole pod, so they can play and feed.

Dolphins have the ability to switch off half their brain,
But unlike our politicians they can turn it on again.

They're also in great shape, I know we cant compete,
They can swim at 40 miles per hour, so they're quite the athlete.

They care for one another, displaying their affection,
They have the rare ability to recognize their reflection.

Dolphins are superior in almost every way,
We're bad for their existence, but I want them to stay.

So I shall look and find a way to help the dolphins live,
I will find a charity, and recommend we give.

https://us.whales.org/whales-dolphins/facts-about-dolphins/

April 15th 2021

Yesterday's dolphin poem had a broken link,
Was it just a blunder or done to make you think.

Well I must confess it was a big mistake
I sent it in the morning, before I was awake.

I hadn't had my coffee yet, so wasn't quite alive,
The future poems will be checked, or at least that's what I strive.

So for those of you who clicked it and got an error page,
I hope you can forgive me, and blame it on my age.

Or blame it on my drowsiness, my semi conscious mode,
I had not fully booted, my OS did not load.

The text itself was accurate, you could have copy pasted,
But if that broken- link you clicked, your time I truly wasted.

April 16th 2021

Here is a poem, about the one I adore
It's full of emotion, and feelings galore.

When they are sad, I become blue
And when they frown, I will frown too.

When they are happy, my smile is wide
When they tell fibs, I know they have lied.

When I smile at them, they smile back,
They know what I'm thinking, it must be a knack.

I love to be with them, their smile, their grin
I love every bit, from their feet to their chin.

Without them I simply, could not exist
When they are not happy, their smile is missed.

I should have declared, who this person be
You all know this person, this person is me.

April 17th 2021

International Haiku Poetry Day

I don't like Haikus, they're not really my thing,
I like the words to bounce, to play and to sing.
A bit more like Seuss, and his cat in the box,
Or maybe that's Schrodinger, now he really rocks.

But today I will try and write a haiku,
They follow some rules not easy to do.
Five syllables sit in line one of three,
Seven come next, then five finally.

So please wish me luck, here is my haiku,
It's not very good, I know that is true.
So judge if you like, but don't make me cry,
When you've done reading this, you give it a try.

Now it's Haiku time,
It's quite hard to make them rhyme,
Not today, I chime.

April 18th 2021

I wonder what my grandson's future will be like?
Will he have a flying car or a hover bike?

Will he play with Lego, or on a P S 20
Cos if he plays with Lego that boy will sure have plenty.

Will they have a holodeck or some other 3D Telly?
Will they still eat fast food or a nutrient jelly?

Will they cure the common cold, or wipe out all the cancers?
Or will we still be wearing masks, I'm sure no one can answer.

April 19th 2021

This is a story of a dolphin named Jake,
He followed the boats and surfed in their wake.

He'd swim and he'd jump and he'd twist in the air,
Jake lived his life like he had no care.

He ate when he wanted, never listened to mum,
He thought he was smart, but really quite dumb.

Never helped with the chores, or cleaned up his home,
Never stayed with the Pod, he just wanted to roam.

Jake was teenager, handsome and fit,
But he was also an arrogant shit.

Then one fateful day he ate too much puffer,
He couldn't control it and started to suffer.

He strayed from the Pod and hung out by the docks,
Now a photo of Jake is on the milk box.

April 20th 2021

Today is April twentieth, thats four-twenty to you,
A day the potheads celebrate, and smoke what they just grew.

They revere the holy hemp plant, inhale the holy smoke,
And giggle uncontrollably when someone tells a joke.

Then they get the munchies and eat up all the grub,
And they keep on smoking all the way down to the stub.

They say it's not that harmful, I'm not sure I agree,
I get the medical benefits, that is plain to see.

But used for recreation, it alters your brain state,
And eating all those munchies is not good for your weight.

April 21st 2021

What will they name him, will it be rare?
An unusual name from an unusual pair.

They might give him a name from a book or movie
Something unique but also quite groovy.

Here are some suggestions, each line is a set.
See how many connections you get.

Nelix, Phlox, Odo, or Spock,
Andre', Cactus or maybe The Rock

Aragon, Gimli, Gollum, or Merry,
Blue Bell, Breyers, or Ben and Jerry.

Eugene, Patrick, Squidward, or Gary,
Eobard, Hunter, Wally, or Barry.

Trillion, Zaphod, Marvin, or Ford,
Duke, Prince, Baron, or Lord.

Jimmy, Carl, Goddard, or Sheen
Lucifer, Balthazar, or Constantine.

Lister, Rimmer, Kryton, or Cat
Leo, Ralph, or Splinter the rat.

Sirius, Draco, Dobby, or Newt,
Yondu, Drax, Rocket, or Groot.

Lando, Yoda, Chewie or Han,
Kal-el, Clark or just Superman

Neo, Morpheus, Cypher, or Tank
Dale, Jeff, Bobby, or Hank

Cohen, Mort, Rincewind, or Death,
Romeo, Yorick, or maybe Macbeth.

So how many groups were easy to spot?
Did you get very few, or get quite a lot?

If they picked one of these I think I would freak,
Whatever they choose, it will be unique.[2]

---

[2] Cheat Sheet on page 147

April 22nd 2021

Earth Day

This globe that we live on, this place we call Earth,
A big ball of mud, it's the place of our birth.

A blue and green sphere with white wispy fluff,
Smooth from a distance, get closer it's rough.

Get closer still and you see the great seas,
The wispy white stuff moves in the breeze.

The jagged land masses of granite and lime,
Created by lava, carved over time.

Get even closer, it's covered in life.
On the land there is plenty, in the oceans it's rife.

The life is diverse, it's a wonder to view,
Some species are old and some are quite new.

On closer inspection it's infested with man,
Go buy some bug spray and buy a big can.

April 23rd 2021

St Georges Day

Today we celebrate George the one who slayed the dragon,
Not the designer of cheap jeans in your Walmart wagon.

He's the patron saint of England, but the story is misleading,
For when you do the research and do some history reading.

You delve into the past, you turn into a sleuth,
You may find out what happened, you may find out the truth.

He really didn't slay a dragon, for dragons don't exist,
It was more than bloody likely the lot of them were pissed.

I don't want to pass on gossip, or a rumor spread,
But this is probably similar to what St George had said.

"I will kill your dragon, I shall slay your beast,
But only if you bow down to my God and to my priest."

This doesn't sound very saintly, it sounds like quid pro quo,
We all know this is frowned upon, it's just a big no no.

April 24th 2021

I filled out a form on the day of my shot
Race was a field, with a line or a slot

I asked, can I write human in here?
She told me no, then grinned ear to ear.

But I wasn't joking, that is my race,
I am not defined by the hue of my face.

Nationality's one thing, color is too
But my race is human, I know that is true.

Will bigots stop hating? Can we all get along?
A human's a human and all types belong.

April 25th 2021

There are people who think the earth is flat, how stupid can they be?
Anyone with half a brain knows it's shaped more like a pea.

If it were flat we'd fall off when over the edge we look,
But maybe these flat earthers, believe they're in a book.

The only world that's plate shaped sits atop four pachyderms
And they ride upon a turtle, through space that turtle worms.

This book is in the library, it's under fantasy,
That's where the other books should go on flat earth conspiracy.

So listen all you wack jobs that think the earth is flat
Go jump off the flipping edge and swim in turtle scat.
[3]

---

[3] Referencing the Discworld Novels by Sir Terry Pratchett

April 26th 2021

Our society is broken, it's corrupt and full of greed,
For the sake of all our children we need to change I plead.

If the money that the world spends on military might,
Were put to better use, the future would be bright.

Instead of needless battles between a few world leaders,
Invest in education, make a nation of succeders.

Stick the leaders in a room and let them fight it out,
Televise the battle and let us cheer and shout.

Our future has two options, It's pretty clear to me,
A Star Trek type utopia or Mad Max society.

One where we advance, past wars and greed and hunger,
The other's where earth's gone to shit, no future for our younger.

April 27th 2021

Mankind is a menace we are killing off our earth
We all need to take heed, for what this warnings worth

Garbage piles are growing, it doesn't decompose,
The mess we're making of our planet really kinda blows.

The pollution rate's expanding, we need it to contract,
The doubters say it's theory, the data says it's fact.

What we're leaving for our children is a giant ball of scrap
For a species that's intelligent we're really kinda crap.

Will mankind stop polluting? Will climate change reverse?
The earth can't take much more of this, we'll need a bigger hearse.

April 28th 2021

All you anti-vaxxers and you antimaskers too,
We know you think the whole world revolves around just you.

If the air you breath was yours, then you might just have a point,
But the air you breathe is shared, I hate to disappoint.

It carries the bad virus that's deadly to some folk,
So don't listen to your leaders, it's really not a joke.

When you rant about your freedom you really sound quite fake,
Put your damn mask on and don't be a big snowflake.

It's your right to go maskless, this may be your view,
But it's my right to clean air, not polluted air from you.

So when your rights infringe on mine which rights do we defy?
Do us all a favor catch the virus and then die.

April 29th 2021

Here's a little poem about Oreo the cat,
You know she's into mischief when you don't know where she's at.

When she came into our home she was a little kitten,
It wasn't very long before all of us were smitten.

She likes to get the laundry and take it to her bowl,
To quench the laundry's thirst was definitely her goal.

She grew up chasing doggies when they got too near,
She'd leave her little claws behind in their nose or ear.

She often had her moments, a friendly ball of fluff,
Addicted to her catnip, she couldn't get enough.

She looks like little hitler with a tiny black moustache,
She often had her crazy time, around the house she'd dash.

She also had a temper with her human pets,
She'd reach out with her sharp claws, if too close they gets.

She likes to sit in boxes if her belly fits
She likes to eat the bubble wrap, it comes out in her shits

She likes to play with ice cubes floating in her drink
I'm sure she likes to sing to them, at least that's what I think.

But now she's getting older and she's getting kinda mellow,
Her eyesight is declining and her belly's turned to jello.

I'm not sure how much longer on this earth she'll be,
But knowing this old ornery cat, she will out live me.

April 30th 2021

This journey through my mind is coming to a close,
I hope I've entertained you all with my offbeat prose.

So this is number 30 the last one of this set
If they all made sense to you, you're crazy too, I bet.

Some ideas come easy, they're explosive in my mind,
Some are slightly harder, the words are hard to find.

My thoughts are fairly jumbled, they dribble out my brain
You may have read my poems and thought, this guy's insane.

Often times a topic is bouncing round my head,
From the moment that I get up, to the time I go to bed.

The words live in my neurons, a small synaptic twinkle,
And if it stays in there too long it becomes another wrinkle.

Once the words have left their home my next task is compile
And I hope that someone reads it and that it makes them smile.

My poems are not super, sometimes they really stink,
But occasionally I'd like them to make the reader think.

So I just get my notepad and let the words just play,
And hope that maybe sometime they make somebody's day.

They say the word is mighty, more so than the sword,
This crazy train's departing, so I say all aboard.

Family

<u>The Ladies of My Life</u>

There are some girls upon this world who I'll love till the end of time,
So to show them just how much I care, I wrote this little rhyme.

My sister cos she helped me through the tough few years of school,
And for showing me that I'm a nerd, but that it's also cool.

There's my mom because she made me and she taught me wrong from right,
She fed me in the daytime and kept me safe when it was night.

There's Whitney cos we made her, of her I'm very proud,
She is the silver lining to my thunder cloud.

Then there is you, the only one I love, that I can say I chose,
I could have picked a thorny stalk, but no, I picked the rose.

Whitney's 18

It's August fifteenth two thousand and eight,
You're eighteen years old, isn't that great?

You can own your own house, you can buy tobacco,
You can drive to Shreveport and lose all your dough.

You can vote, you can marry, you can work in a bar,
You can get a tattoo without permission from pa.

Now you're grown-up you have so much to do,
Just remember that Mummy and Daddy love you.

Whitney Jade - A Monkey's Tale

Twenty One Years of Whitney Jade
To celebrate this, a poem I've made.

It starts with a baby, so happy and cute
Her first word was 'nana, the curved yellow fruit.

She got mummy's looks, so she has been blessed
She got daddy's hands, maybe not the best.

She got common sense from the mummy-half
But she got daddy's humor; at herself, she can laugh.

She always seemed happy, and crying didn't last
She was growing up quickly, in fact way too fast.

She thought she was too old to be wearing her nappy
But carrying that ketchup pack, that made her happy.

She sat in her Poopchair[4] and asked to go fast
He pushed her quite quickly, but it didn't last.

She said "Faster, daddy," daddy's starting to pant
"I'm running as fast as I can," "well run as fast as you can't!"

Even back then she had an art flare
A saddle on Arnie made out of a chair.

Her head a pinano[5], and so was her nose
She started with a keyboard, but cello she chose.

Next came the Brownies and a trip to the chippy
Where the greasy old chips were bendy and drippy.

Then there were long days of Choir and school
With a small stone carved imp and a statue of Boole.

Moving to Texas is next in the tale
Where Art would now flourish, but Math would now fail.

Without Math, what would happen to Miss Whitney Jade?
We need after-class tutors to bring up the grade.

Then high school was better, with Art now her focus
None of that Math stuff; that's hocus pocus.

---

[4] Poopchair is what she called her pushchair
[5] Pinano is what she called a piano

Drawing and playing The Sims was now it
And maybe she thought about boys quite a bit.

And one other thing that I nearly forgot
Something that Whitney loves quite a lot.

I knew I'd missed something then it started to dawn
It's her kitty cat Oreo, a.k.a. Devils Spawn.

She studied Karate, a thing best forgotten
She leaves all her dishes to go moldy and rotten.

She doesn't like veggies and she doesn't like fruit
And she doesn't like daddy when he lets out a toot.

Through High School she grew, in talent not size
She made lots of friends; some girls and some guys.

Some have drifted away, but all glad to have met
They are part of her life so their own stanza they get.

One with a head that's shaped like a melon
One that could possibly end up a felon.

One with a Mohawk, one joined the marines
One's supposed to be doctor, but he's stacking baked beans.

She likes her stuffed toys, especially gorillas
They sit on her bed in between all the pillows.

She sleeps on her front with her cat on her bum
And she talks in her sleep, but then so does her mum.

She learnt how to drive in her dad's yellow Jeep
Around the school car park slowly she'd creep.

And now she rides buses and trams, and street cars
And she's old enough now to go into bars.

She likes to drive fast, when no one is looking
She likes to bake cookies, well she likes all the cooking.

But she doesn't like washing the dishes one bit
And she doesn't like cleaning out the cat shit.

She likes Vampire movies and Reality Shows
Why she likes all this stuff, nobody knows.

She likes Sandler and Schneider, and Will Ferrell too
Her fave color is green, but it used to be blue.

She has a good sense of humor and cool sense of style
Pretty brown eyes and big cheesy smile.

She can get her own way with that puppy dog look
But she sure does have a mean right hook!

Now let's talk about jobs, those future and past
There were those that she liked, and those that didn't last.

Electronics and Clothing and Portraits were crappy
But after-school children, now they made her happy.

The future is bright with so much to choose
Whatever you pick, I'm sure you can't lose.

Printmaker, Artist, Gallery Owner
There's one thing I'm sure, you won't end up a stoner.

You could be a Book Binder, you could be a Writer
But I don't recommend an MMA Fighter.

You could be a model, you could be a Teacher
Another bad choice might just be a Preacher.

It's time to wrap up this poem I've written
So from mummy and me, and cat, dog and kitten.

We wish you the best in your year twenty two
Happy Birthday dear Whitney, you know we love you!

My Mum

Who would feed and burp me and change me when I hum
There's only one who'd dare do that, and her name is "My mum"

Who would let me stay home when I had a painful tum
There's only one who'd even care, and her name is "My mum"

Who would stand behind me when teachers called me dumb
There's only one who finks I is smart, and her name is "My mum"

Who's the best cook in the world, corned beef stew, yum yum
There's only one who knows how it's made, and her name is "My mum"

Who smacked my butt when I was bad, till it became real numb
There's only one who could get close, and her name is "My mum"

Who would hug me even though I look like a street bum
There's only one who'd love this face, and her name is "My mum"

A Poem for Dad

Dads are pretty special, you only get one dad
They're mostly an embarrassment, and their jokes are always bad.

To stop the fights, they claim the last slice of the cake
But even on the first round, the biggest piece they take.

Far too many hammers, and tins of nails and screws
And cans of dried old paint, with tubs of hardened glues.

Getting mad at stupid stuff, that entertained us tonnes
Like hopping on the driveway, cos your gas tank had the runs.

Getting very sunburnt, cos you didn't use sunscreen
Then being called a bunch of names, cos your family's very mean.

Take the success of the children to measure greatness of the dad
I guess you did ok, because one out of three aint bad ;)

Father's Day

It's Father's Day again, so I thought I'd write some ditties,
to the dad parental unit, that's the one without the titties.

You taught me quite a bit of stuff while I was just a nipper,
like when you finish peeing, don't get caught inside the zipper.

You taught me which direction, that I should turn a screw,
You taught me which end of the hammer, I should hold on to.

You taught me right from wrong, and that grey bit in between,
You taught me how to make home-brew when I was just a teen.

You taught me that the dad jokes were just you being clever,
And that I would use them cos there timeless and forever.

You taught me how to shake a hand the first time you say hello,
You taught me not to eat the snow, especially when it's yellow.

You taught me about anger, and the damage it can do,
Especially to the clothing that you bit a hole right through.

You taught me how to ride a bike, and how to stop and go,
You taught me how to scream and yell at the drivers going slow,

You taught me lots of useful stuff, for which I thank you tonnes,
Like making carts, fixing bikes, and building rubber-band guns.

So Mahalo Nui Loa from the flip side of the earth,
I thank you most of all for that event I call "my birth".

Cathay's Birthdays

Not all the poems are contained in this book. Mostly because the originals got lost, but it may also be because the content of them

Happy 40th Birthday Cathy

Forty years since you were born, it may seem a lot to you
But think of it in generations, now it's less than 2.

Think of it in leap years and now it's only 10,
So you're not happy with that one too, I will think on it again.

But think of it in hex and it's only 28
Surely that one's pretty good, surely that one's great.

Now look at me at 43, I think that that sounds plenty
Take a look in months now and it's five hundred and twenty.

Now what if you'd been born on Mars, how old would you be then
The answer to that's pretty good, it's two one point two seven.

So let's take this one step further, and view the facts again,
Women are from Venus and Mars is home to Men.

That makes you over sixty five and makes me twenty two
Now who's robbing cradles, ha ha, I think it's you.

Happy Birthday

Happy birthday to my wife,
You are my world, you are my life.

You mean everything to me,
Without you there would be no we.

For you my left arm I'd give,
For you are my reason to live.

I'd climb a mountain, or sail a sea,
To have you standing here with me.

I'd run 10 miles and win the race,
So I could see your smiling face.

I'd swim the ocean full of man-eating fish,
So I could grant your every wish.

So remember this when I make you sad,
I must have gone temporarily mad.

I love you Cathy, with all my heart,
My greatest wish - we never part.

Happy 42nd

It's that time of the year, when I sit and write verse,
You're probably thinking each year it gets worse,

It's hard to come up with all these words that rhyme,
Some poems are quick, some poems take time.

So sorry if this one is not up to par,
If you want my opinion, not many are,

I will try to do better for the one due next week,
In the middle of that one, right now, as we speak.

This one's for your birthday, now you're forty two,
So the rhymes in this poem have got to be new,

So out of my ass my head I must pull,
And put pen to paper until it is full.

Forty two is a really cool age to be at,
Well if you're a human, not if you're a cat.

It's one of my favorite numbers you see.
But then you know that, because you know me.

I hope that your birthday's as fun as can be,
As fun as it can be shackled to me,

So continue to party and have a good time,
While I stall for a while to find words that might rhyme.

Well I found some words that I might want to use,
These words are quite special; I don't want to lose,

These words are just perfect, I think they're ideal
They are what I think, they are what I feel.

Three little words that are always worthwhile,
Three little words that can make you smile,

Three little words that are coming from me
These three little words are "Cup of Tea?"

47th

You open the card and what do you see,
An L and an h stare back at me.

An L and an h, what does it mean?
The strangest message I've ever seen.

An L and an h, just what is this code?
A secret admirer, my heart will explode.

What is the meaning, I really can't see.
My confusion doesn't last as she reads it to me..

It's only a birthday card no hidden note,
So what was the L and h someone had wrote?

You'll think me a ninny, when you find out you see
It was no L or h staring back at me.

From where I was sitting the card was inverted,
No reason for my poor little brain to be hurted.

Just turn over the letters they're letters no more,
The L is a seven, the h is a four.

Lh = 47

Cathy's Poem Birthday 2017

Oh my god you're 48, you really are quite old,
Your hair is going gray, and your skin's begun to fold,

Your bone creaks are quite deafening, and your walking pace is slow,
Your sight's too bad to see yourself, so I'm not sure if you know.

So as you're very old now, I've got some good advice,
Like drying out wet hearing aids, inside a bag of rice,

Or taking notebooks with you, to write down all your lists,
Or take a break when typing, or you'll end up with sore wrists.

We'll have to trade your paddle in, for a walking stick or cane,
We'll have to buy Alzheimer meds, to help your aging brain,

We'll have to buy some hair dye, to hide away the gray,
We'll have to buy some caffeine, to stop you snoozing in the day.

Getting old can be quite bad, forgetting who you are,
We'll have to put a leash on you, so you don't stray too far,

But even though you're getting old, and your body's wearing out,
I would pick you again and again of that I have no doubt.

The Big Five-Oh

Fifty's just a number, it's no big deal you say,
An arbitrary number of an arbitrary day.

But that's not really true you see, it really is quite cool,
It's fifty years from diapers and fifty years from drool.

So why is it a milestone, is it overrated?
Why is the number 50 quite so celebrated?

You're into your sixth decade, it really is quite neat,
Compared to the dark ages it's really quite a feat.

Their average life expectancy was only twenty nine,
If you lived till you were 40 you were doing rather fine.

So you made it to that ripe old age of half a century,
You've joined me in this decade, now you're catching up with me.

It's eighteen thousand days plus another two six two
That equates to fifty days of just sitting on the loo.

Now that's a lot of poop, even for someone so fit,
When you add it all together, it's five metric tonnes of shit.

This poem's not very nice, it's not what you expected,
It probably won't get stored with all the others you've collected.

Happy 51st Birthday!

A happy birthday poem to put a smile upon your face,
A birthday gift to unwrap, a gift that's kinda ace.

A piece of Cake to gobble, after blowing out the flames,
A strip tease in the bedroom by a hunky dude called James.

Now maybe that's a white lie, this James is pretty fat,
But when he's finished dancing, he'll be wearing just his hat.

He's also kinda old now, so the dance may be quite slow,
His bladder isn't what it was, so he'll need a break you know.

Then tired from the dancing he'll probably need a sleep,
That's when you open prezzies, and see that I am cheap.

Let's hope the cake and icecream will be a bigger hit,
Cos if it's not, that James guy, well he'll be in the shit.

Fifty one is not that old, it's not like fifty four,
Is that James still sleeping, can you hear him snore?

That James should put the kettle on, so go wake up that codger,
But make sure he gets dressed first, so he dont burn his todger.

Valentines Poems

This chapter of poems were written to my wife. Not all the poems are contained in this book. The original got lost, or she claimed they got lost because they contain content that may be too personal and might embarrass her.

Valentine Poem

Add to one couple some feelings of bliss,
One pound of forever, a hug and a kiss.

A pint and a half of enchanting smile,
Stir in some passion and let sit for a while.

A cup full of soul with a half pound of dance,
A teaspoon of love and a dash of romance.

Some soul blended in with a quart of embrace,
Mix it together and add spice to taste.

Coat baking tray with some tenderness
And pipe out the mixture but don't make a mess.

Now cover and bake for a lifetime or more
But once in the oven don't open that door.

St Valentine

Long ago there lived a guy
Called Valentine, and that's no lie.

His goal in life was plain to see,
Spread the word of love to folks like me.

One legend says, back in century three,
He risked his life keeping romance free.

He lived in Rome, where he was a priest,
All marriages the Emperor had ceased.

He broke the law and performed the wedding,
His last performance was his own beheading.

I don't know if this story's right,
Maybe my version will shed some light.

He wrote the poems for Hallmark Inc.
He drew the hearts of red and pink.

He collected toys, all soft and fluffed,
He loved his chocolate, strawberry stuffed.

He loved diamond jewelry, he loved flowers too,
He loved long hot baths, with sweet smelling shampoo.

He likes to read books of romance and passion
He actually has a keen sense of fashion.

Now wait a minute, this guy's not right
I think he wears his jeans too tight.

Valentine 2005

A rainbow of colors is my love for you,
It's red and it's orange, it's green and it's blue.

The blue is the times that we have a fight,
But it doesn't last long, pretty soon it's alright.

The yellow's a bumpy drive down the street,
A road we call life, this one I can't beat.

Green is for money, we've been broke, we've been poor,
But with you I am rich, could not ask for more.

Pink is for all of the girls in my life,
My daughter, my mom, my pets and my wife.

Orange is like the big sun in the sky,
It's hot just like you, it's round just like I.

The purple's for bruises I get them in bed,
When I'm snoring at night and you elbow my head.

Indigo is for blue jeans that we wear,
Always together, always a pair.

But today it is red, 'cause it is Valentine's Day,
A day I'm reminded, I love you any old way.

Valentine 2007

To you this Valentine poem I write,
Hoping that it will shed some light.

It's Valentine 's Day 2007,
Each moment with you is still like heaven.

We've been together over half my life,
And I'm still happy that you're my wife.

22 years since we started to date,
That's not just good, that's bloody great.

I love you this much, written on a heart,
I knew back then, we'd never part.

Beggar kitty, pup and bunny,
I bought you stuff with borrowed money.

We'd go skating Saturday night,
Sometimes left and sometimes right.

But most of the time we'd just sit down,
I'd gaze into your eyes so brown.

Head over heels, I fell for you,
Now you're stuck with me like gorilla glue.

I am so lucky that you said yes,
Without you around I'd be a mess.

Now it's years later, and I still go weak
When you're in the shower, and I have a peek.

It won't be long before were old and grey,
As we sit in our swing on the porch, and sway.

Or maybe a beach on the island of Maui
You can kiss my boo boos, I'll kiss your owie.

Wherever we are, I know I'll love you,
Thanks to that night when I drank my homebrew.

Valentine 2011

So here it is another valentine day,
A time when its common to hear people say,

I love you, be mine and you are my life,
Or even propose and say please be my wife.

But that is not I, for the reason is clear,
I do not save my words for one day a year.

I love you as much each and every day,
Not just in February, not just in May.

I love you no more because today has a name
I will love you next week or next month just the same.

I may not remind you every day,
But I love you as much even if I don't say.

And as each day goes by and I ponder my life,
I am so very thankful that you are my wife.

So never forget, even if I'm not near,
I love you on every day of the year.

Valentine 2016

Green is for Cabbage
Purple for Taro
Little Cupid is aiming
His sharp pointy Arrow.

Red is for Target
Blue for Walmart
That little sharp Arrow
Is deep in my heart.

My boxers are white
A Scott's kilt is plaid
You must be my Valentine
Or I will get sad.

Some jewelry is silver
Some jewelry is gold
Please be my valentine
Before I get Old.

Red is for Tulip
Yellow for Daisy
You must be my valentine
Or I will go Crazy.

Valentine 2017 - This poem stinks but you don't.

Purple and silver and orange don't rhyme,
But red rhymes with lots, well most of the time.

It does till a Valentine poem you write,
And you get stuck on a word, try as you might.

So you switch out the word and replace it with pink
But the rest of the poem is starting to stink.

So change it again to cherry or rose,
This poem gets worse, in the trash can it goes.

We start it again this time without color
It goes a bit better, although it is duller.

So another scrunched paper goes into the bin
My brain starts to hurt, my head starts to spin.

Maybe I'll sleep on it, and give it a rest,
That's when the poems I write are the best.

So tonight I will record myself while I'm asleep
We'll see what we get while I'm counting the sheep.

Some snoring, and farting, how romantic am I?
This valentine poem is making me cry.

I'm having some trouble finding the word,
This valentine poem is stinking like turd.

Just one more verse before I call it a day,
A final remark that I need to say.

This poem may suck, it may stink like poo,
But when all's said and done, I really love you!

Valentines 2018

I sit at my keyboard from morning to night,
One mushy poem my intention to write.

The emotions and feelings are stuck in my mind,
The words don't come out, they're too hard to find.

So I take a quick break, on Facebook I browse,
Through pictures of you with horses and cows.

Of you on the water, a paddle in hand,
Or sat in a deckchair upon the white sand.

Videos of dolphins are scattered throughout,
The odd picture of whales and their waterspout.

I look back still further and see pictures of ships,
Cruisy cruise photos of us on our trips.

These memories of good times all shine through the screen,
The happy adventures and places we've been.

I look back so fondly of our fun filled life,
So lucky and happy that you are my wife.

I love you as much as the day we were wed,
I will love you forever, well at least till I'm dead.

Valentine 2019

Do animals love, or is it just us?
What's love all about, what is all this fuss?

If aliens visited us in their ship,
What would they learn about us on their trip?

Love is not limited to humans you see,
It's felt by the animals across land and sea.

The cats with their purr, the dogs wagging tails,
Birds mourning lost ones, families of whales.

We see it around, but we don't pay attention,
Hallmark write the cards, but they don't get a mention.

The critters love too, it's quite plain to see,
They often love more than the humans like me.

So let's take a moment to look at the planet,
This big round blue marble of water and granite.

A shout out for nature, hip hip hooray,
Their love is all year, not one stupid day.

Valentine's 2020 - That's what love is!

Being together through thick and thin
While the sight of you still makes me grin
That's what love is!

Listening to me going on about shit
Paying attention when you don't care a bit
That's what love is!

Eating greens and healthy food
You not laughing when I'm in the nude
That's what love is!

Taking care of your man, when he's got the man flu
Walking two dogs carrying bags full of poo
That's what love is!

A small emoji upon my phone
A wagging tail to an egg filled bone
That's what love is!

Feeling the guilt when I dont buy a gift
Go on a cruise and not once take a lift
That's what love is!

Doing more than your share of all the chores
Like washing the dishes or sweeping the floors
That's what love is!

Watching political crap on streaming TV
When there's yard work to do like moving a tree
That's what love is!

Putting up with my twaddle and my diatribe
A few times a year, a poem I scribe
That's what love is!

Nagging at me when I keep saying no
So you turn to a bribe, it's not quid pro quo
That's what love is!

Ooops, What Gift Did I buy?

A dozen roses, a box of chocs,
A diamond ring, a pair of socks,

So many gifts I could buy for you.
Too many choices, what am I to do?

It's Valentine's day, so maybe a cupid,
So what do I get? I get something stupid.

Cupid has arrows and an aim that is fair,
So what do I get? A Robin Hood bear.

But that's not the worst, what else do I find?
Something taboo, something unkind.

An exercise disc that knows what you weigh,
But it isn't silent, to the world it must say.

A reprieve I might have, cos I have just thought,
I've no need to worry about what I have bought,

It's me that's the fatty, she's pretty and thin,
So give her the gift, and don't be a nin.

Endless Love

My love for you is endless
It just goes on and on.

Just like an Eveready battery
Or a darn Eminem song.

I love you when your happy
I love you when you're sad.

I love you when your grumpy
Or even when you're mad.

I'll love you when you're old and grey
I'd love you with no hair.

Id love you if you were senile
Or in a wheelchair.

I'd love you if you killed me
Or something even wronger.

I'll love you for eternity
Or maybe even longer.

So just to show you that it's true
And to end this little rhyme.

I vow to love you always
Until the end of time.

Anniversary Poems

Not all the poems I have written to her for our anniversary are contained in this book. Some were too crude, too personal, or the original got lost.

Anniversary 2004

Sixteen years of marriage is just a preface to
A literary masterpiece that features me and you.

It starts with teenage sweethearts and follows them through their life
Telling stories of adventures for this husband and his wife.

The first adventure was the wedding with the tails and top hat
And the party afterwards with a gate crasher, a rat.

The honeymoon started off separated by an aisle
As time went by the trip improved and both of them did smile.

A few months later they found out they were going to have a child
They sold their house and moved abroad and then their lives got wild.

Their new home was much warmer than the place they had come from
They had their child, it was a girl as pretty as her mom.

The years went by and every day they loved each other more
Even through the good and bad, the rich times and the poor

Now they fight quite often, but it's only friendly fun
Their fighting in the living room, their fighting in the sun.

But this fighting isn't vicious or meant to hurt or scar
They're practicing their hobby, a family of karate ka.

Some people find it difficult to work at married life
But it's really quite simple when the one you're with is my wife.

Anniversary 2005

17 years of wedded bliss
And it all started with a drunken kiss.

My mouth stuffed with chocolate cake
A little bit more than my stomach could take.

The air filled with romance, or was it my vomit
Years ago before Wallace and Gromitt.

It may have got off to a pretty bad start
But ever since then you've a place in my heart.

With my head in the clouds and your feet on the ground
We make a good team, you skinny, me round.

You put up with my habits, my farting and snoring
You put up with me when I'm totally boring.

We've argued and fought, you've gone off in a huff
But think of the fun that we've had in the buff.

30 more years I'll be old, fat and bald
Kind of like now but now I'm less old.

You will still be the love of my life
I'll still be your husband, you'll still be my wife.

Anniversary 2006

Looking' back it's plain to see,
Just why the heck you stuck with me.

A lapse in judgment, Cupid's dart,
A touch of madness, a dang brain fart.

It was temporary insanity
That made you fall in love with me.

Looking' back it's plain to see,
Just why the heck I fell for thee.

The hottest bod I ever knew,
That saved me from my own home brew.

From monkey boots to fuzzy head,
I knew back then that we would wed.

For many years I've grown to see,
That you're insane and I'm lucky.

Anniversary 2008

It's been twenty years since our wedding day,
If it hasn't sunk in yet, I am here to stay.

You were warned by my mom; you were warned by my dad,
"If you marry our kid, you really are mad".

Two hundred and forty months of "we"
A thousand and forty weeks of glee.

Ten million minutes of wedded bliss
And it all started out with a drunken kiss.

I love you as much as the day that we wed,
I will love you as much till the day we are dead.

Words can't express just how much I love you
So I'm adding a drawing and I hope it will do.

It may not be great, but it's quite plain to see
That you are the only person for me.

You are smart, you are funny, you are pretty and kind
Just what did I do to get such a find?

I've said it before; I'll say it a new
If I had it to do over, I'd still say "I Do".

Anniversary 2011

No traditional gift for year twenty three,
So I was thinking of putting a bow around me.

I wanted to give you something that's nice,
But stick to the budget, be careful of price.

Nice but no money, now that's hard to find,
I'll give that Dave Ramsey a piece of my mind.

So what should I get for the world's best wife?
I will give her the thing I like best in this life.

So the gift I will give you, I will try to explain
Comes not from the heart, but straight from my brain

That image of beauty, that wonderful view,
That comes through my eyes when I'm looking at you.

The love that I feel when I'm hugging you tight
That waggy tail feeling when you come home at night.

The sound of your laughter, the smile on your face,
The feel of your skin on a Friday embrace.

But above all those feelings there's one that stands out
I'll love you forever and of that there's no doubt.

Anniversary 2015

27 years since you walked down the aisle,
and we spent the whole day being ordered to smile.

A reception slow dance, and an apple pie bed,
a night of romance, a flight to the Med.

Pork from a pig that ate prickly pear,
A beach where old ladies were lying half bare.

A few of my thoughts as I look back in time,
As I write you this poem, an anniversary rhyme.

Other moments of note from our years of spousal,
a moment of extra clean bathtub arousal.

The official news of your fertilization,
Our trip overseas, my lack of vocation.

The birth of our child, the miss Whitney Jade,
Something that perfect that we had both made.

Skipping over some verses to jump to the now,
Where I work with houses and you work with cow.

I live on an island with the the love of my life,
On the side of a mountain, here with my wife.

I can honestly say I'm the luckiest guy,
My heart is yours till the day that I die.

Anniversary 2016

Tight blue jeans, and monkey boots too.
Bleached blonde fringe the rest number two.

Black cardigan with thumb holes in sleeves.
Just some of the things from my memories.

Round and around the roller skate rink.
Parties at youth clubs with too much to drink.

Head over heels I was starting to fall.
Just some of the things that I can recall.

A canvas bag tattered and scorched.
Holes from a penny that had been torched.

Evenings of bliss that went way too fast
Just some of the things I have in my past.

A trip on a canal with your mom and dad.
A stroll in the woods that wasn't too bad.

An occasional break up, I'd end up in tears.
Just some of the things I've done through the years.

I'd pick you up in a yellow sports car.
We'd go for a drive but we wouldn't go far.

How did I do it, it's a mystery.
Just some of the things in my history.

We picked out the rings, we picked out the date.
The wedding was awesome, the honeymoon great.

But this wasn't the end of the perfect romance.
This was the start of the perfect dance.

Anniversary 2017

Twenty nine years that we have been wed,
Twenty nine years since those words I said.

The ones where I promise a whole bunch of stuff,
Some of it easy and some of it tough.

But no matter the bad times, the sickness or strife,
I would ask you again, would you be my wife.

These days it's not common for two to stay one,
The days of devotion of couples are gone.

I remember my vows, and they still hold true,
I have kept my promise since I said, I Do.

To have and to hold, "have" may not be often,
But I promise to try until we're in our coffin.

For better, for worse, so far has been great,
But that is because you are my best mate.

For richer, for poorer, well we have been broke,
So it's about time we tried out the life of rich folk.

In sickness and health, well right now we're healthy,
Can we try out the sick piece after the wealthy.

To love and to cherish, well that one is easy,
But you're easy to love, I know, that sounds cheesy.

I would renew my vows if you wanted me to,
But I dont think it's needed, as they feel brand new.

Anniversary 2018

Since we got married, we've travelled quite far,
Like thirty round trips that circle our star.

So this special occasion, six gifts I bestow,
The first on the list has cost me no dough.

I hereby release you, from our pet-free accord,
No more waiting a year, no more getting bored.

So when Oreo's gone and you must fill that gap,
Don't wait twelve more months, with an empty lap.

To use gift number two, you first must agree,
The responsible party can not be me.

You don't have to wait till Oreo's pau,
To get a new Cat, Dog, Goat, or Cow.

I get to name it, no matter how weird,
Something like Beast, so it will be feared.

Gift number three, is a week of pet sitting,
When you see number four you will think it quite fitting.

Gift number four to be redeemed at your leisure,
It's a flight to go see your number one treasure.

You pick the time, an occasion or not,
You could go when it's cold, you could go when it's hot.

Now on to unwrapping for the next little gift,
You don't like fine jewelry, so I hope you're not miffed.

Gift number six is both yummy and nice,
Pulled pork, egg, and gravy, on a bed of white rice.

Misc Poems For Cathy

I'm The Luckiest Man Alive

I gaze across the room, you sit there reading your e-book,
It could be the back-lit kindle or maybe it's the nook.

Manini's on your lap, snuggled up into a ball,
A tiny little gecko is walking up the wall.

Oreo's in her bowl, grumbling in her sleep,
Baby birds in the hibiscus, learning how to cheep.

My gaze wanders through the front door, over the lanai,
Out to deep blue ocean that meets the pale blue sky.

I'm the luckiest man alive now, fate has been too kind,
This perfect place, a perfect wife, I can't believe my mind.

We wake up in the morning, it's been raining over night,
The rain has stopped, it's drying up, the weather is just right.

We sit upon our two-man, paddling in the sun,
Watching all the dolphins, out there having fun.

An hour or two of paddling then meet up for some brunch,
Then home to play with puppy, and all this before lunch.

A trip out in the truck to the dump or to the shops,
Then a stop for a quick break to get our sody pops.

I'm the luckiest man alive now, fate has been too kind,
This perfect place, a perfect wife, I can't believe my mind.

Oranges, Bananas, Passion Fruit, and the Stars,
All of this is growing in this garden that is ours.

Black and green sand beaches, and lava rock galore,
Palm trees and plumeria, all at our backdoor.

Shorts and t-shirt weather every single day,
It can not get much better in any single way.

A car, a Jeep, a truck, two bikes, and three canoes,
A closet full of costumes, a house with perfect views.

I'm the luckiest man alive now, fate has been too kind,
This perfect place, a perfect wife, I can't believe my mind.

About Me

I'm Getting Old

Here's a little ditty for all of you out there,
I am getting older, I'm losing all my hair.

Well, the hair upon my head is what I seem to lack,
But I have an abundance growing on my back.

The hair upon my chin is going kinda grey,
And now it grows so fast it needs shaving twice a day.

My eyesight's getting fuzzy, my hearing's going too,
I spend a lot more time just running to the loo.

My laughter lines are spreading, they've discovered how to clone,
They won't stop multiplying, sprouting branches of their own.

My eyebrows are quite wild, they're also going grey,
My testicles are pendulous, they're getting in the way.

My temper's getting shorter, along with other things,
All of this, I guess, is what getting older brings.

My memory is going, it really is a pity
What was it I was doing? oh yes, I'll write a ditty.

No Special Occasion - I'm Just Special!

Sometimes I write you poetry as a sign of my affection.
Or I may write a poem when my thought's in deep reflection.

It might be about my love, or my horny bod desire.
But I always write the truth, in my poems I'm no liar.

So I wrote you one to celebrate our thirty years together.
Richer, poorer, sickness, health, in awful or good weather.

The poem was a gift list, of all the things you'd get
One of which was letting you off our agreement about a pet

Then one day at Micky D's, while ordering our drinks
We saw the puppy's puppy's mom and I began to think

If I wait until the right time to hand over the list
She'll miss out on the opportunity and then she might be pissed

So I let you read it early because the time was right.
An action that I might regret while we get up twice a night.

But Manini is a sweety, when she's not biting at our toes.
Or when she leaves us presents, or sticks her tongue right up my nose.

So I guess we've got another kid that tears around the house.
A little barky terror, not much bigger than a mouse.

It hasn't quite sunk in yet, the level I screwed up.
When I made that odd decision to let you have the pup.

These small dogs live to twenty, that makes me seventy two.
So to those pet free dreams I say, sayonara, ciao, adieu.

My Book

Life is just a story, from conception till we die.
Sometimes we want to laugh out loud, sometimes we want to cry.

Sometimes it's kinda boring, sometimes it's kinda fun.
Sometimes it's at a walking pace, sometimes it's at a run.

Some stories are quite lonely, and some are filled with folk.
Some are constant drama, and some are one big joke.

Some are fairly short, and some are giant tomes.
Some are filled with space aliens, and some with tiny gnomes.

Mine's under science fiction, not in with science fact,
Sometimes it's in the self-help, under "How you shouldn't act"

It sits amongst the comic books, with speech bubbles of ZAP.
But almost all my bubbles are filled with stupid crap.

Sometimes my book is hardbound, sometimes it's paperback,
Sometimes with color pictures, sometimes just white and black.

Sometimes it has a typo, sometimes the spelling's wrong.
Sometimes it has a run-on, which makes it very long.

Sometimes it gets mis-filed, on the shelf with religious stuff.
But I'd prefer it on the top shelf, with people in the buff.

You may find it in the kid books, with a book about an elf.
But you'll always find a copy up on the bargain shelf.

All stories have beginnings, they also all have ends.
What's important are the readers, those connections we call friends.

They're with you on this journey, this thing that we call life.
But the most important reader is that one I call my wife.

Miscellaneous

Marriage

Marriage is built on give and take,
Some compromise does happiness make.

Read the signs, know when they're grumpy,
Or you'll be going without your humpy pumpy.

Now we've been married nineteen years,
But it's not been without a couple of tears.

We've had some up's we've had some down's,
We've had some smiles we've had some frowns.

We've had some fights but they don't last long,
I've just gotta remember, I'm usually wrong.

Covid 19 You Suck

Covid 19 you suck, you tiny ball of hate.
You've messed with the wrong species, we'll get you just you wait.

You're an ugly little virus, you think you're really bad.
But you ain't nothing special, you're not the worst we've had.

The Plague killed half of Europe, now that is how you spread.
And Smallpox was a nastie, three hundred million dead.

Now go away you little git, stop picking on our old.
For you're a little coward, with aspirations of a "cold".

We'll just wash our hands, and stand six feet apart,
We won't let you wipe us out, cos some of us are smart.

If I Catch Covid-19

If I catch Covid-19, how would I behave?
Would I start to panic, or would I act all brave?

If I catch Covid-19, would I tell anyone?
Or would I keep it secret, till after I was gone?

If I catch Covid-19, will anybody care?
I'd pick 10 people I don't like and covid I would share.

If I catch Covid-19, would I show any markers?
I might take all my clothes off and run completely starkers.

Quick Poem

Get up at 9 get a bite to eat
Take a stroll through the park then rest my feet

Watch a little TV then get some lunch
Its too early for that so well call it brunch

Play some cards and go for a swim
Have a couple of drinks with some salt round the brim

Eat a late lunch and watch more TV
Boy this seems just like heaven to me

Getting Old

Age is all in the mind, until you get old,
Then the joints start to creak and the skin starts to fold.

The eyesight gets worse and the hearing does too,
And you spend way more time heading off to the loo.

You can try to stay healthy, by eating just right,
And staying quite active, but it's a hell of a fight.

No more lazy weekends, no more ice cream treats,
No more cookies or candy, no more processed meats.

It's downhill from here, that's what they all say,
But I say, not happening, not me, and no way.

I won't wither quietly, getting deaf, blind and slow,
It's not going to happen, I'm not going to go.

I will act like a child, make sure I have fun,
Why walk with the wheels, when you able to run.

Smile and laugh at the things all around,
For one day we won't be here, we'll be 6 feet underground.

We'll be gone, just a memory, inside someone's head
So make sure you enjoy life before you are dead

Live life to the fullest, enjoy every day.
Eat healthy, stay active, but more importantly play.

About Poems

It's poem time of year again,
When words that rhyme bounce around in my brain.

Then line at a time they squirm their way out,
Finding room on the paper, where they try to shout.

The words maybe funny, or filled with romance,
They may make you laugh, they may make you dance.

Occasionally crude, occasionally witty,
They usually rhyme, but are rarely pretty.

Sometimes they have meaning, sometimes they do not,
Some follow a story, some have no plot.

They range from birthdays, to love, onto smut,
Some come from the heart, some out of my butt.

Some are quite short ones, and some are quite long,
Some just a chorus, some a whole song,

But this one is different, it ends quite abrupt.

Polycephaly

You have one head,
Zaphod has two,

Cerberus has three heads,
Fluffy did too.

Lernaean Hydra has five heads,
Scylla has one more,

Typhon has a hundred,
But wait I missed out four.

I couldn't find a monster,
whose headcount numbers four,

But my heads quite gigantic,
It can't fit through the door.

Cupid Stunt

One of those fae creatures must be to blame
You better be careful, I'll tell you his name.

I'm not talking dragon, or even a fairy,
Nor bigfoot or yeti, it's even more scary.

Not Pixie or Sprite, Goblin, or Gnome
This dastardly fae comes into your home.

I trusted my fae friend, I really was stupid
to trust in a person whose name is just Cupid

Oh Cupid you fiend, why fire your dart
right into the center of my soft squishy heart.

He fired again, wait that is not fair,
But this one passed by just grazing my hair.

He fired another, I dive to the ground,
It stuck in my head, gigantic and round.

Another is fired, but whizzed past my butt,
It bounced of the wall and lodged in my left nut.

No matter how many of your arrows that hit
It won't make a difference, not one little bit

I'm already taken, already in love
With a girl who's named Cathy, she fits like a glove.

So keep shooting your arrows, they're just a small prick,
Hey that's kinda like me, with regard to my dick.

Question What You're Told

Question what you're told, it isn't always true,
Sometimes the lies they tell you are nothing more than poo.

Just because you read it, in a book or magazine,
It may not be that factual, the truth could be quite lean.

Some believe in aliens, and some believe in god.
But if I had to choose one, the gray ones get my nod.

Super powers are not real, but it depends on how you scale
Husane Bolt, the fastest man, is super to a snail.

Be careful what you trust in, the truth is hard to see.
But there is a person you can trust, that person it is me.

Me is not the writer of the poem that you scan,
Me is who is reading, that singular human.

Question what they tell you, it may not be a fact.
People try to hide the truth behind a great big act.

The News is mostly biased, it's always got a slant,
It's somebody's opinion, some crazy person's rant.

Take a grain or pinch of salt with everything you read,
Is it really honest, or is it twisted by their greed?

The truth is usually buried within the pile of crap
But be careful what you fall for, it might just be a trap.

My Marvelous Poem

A wall crawling school kid in red spandex.
A professor whose name begins with an X.
An iron suit with gadgets galore.
A teenage girl who can phase through the floor.

A girl who controls rain, snow, and sleet.
A guy who's remarkably quick on his feet.
A god with a hammer, a guy with a shield.
An invisible girl who can form a force field.

A guy who moves metal with the will of his mind.
A lawyer who kicks ass, except he is blind.
A guy who is green with incredible strength.
A man who can stretch to a fantastic length.

A day walking vampire, who's good with a sword.
A group of space outlaws who's lead by a lord.
A merc who can heal and break the fourth wall.
A guy who can shrink or grow really tall.

A girl who can shrink, but she also flies.
A guy who shoots force beams out of his eyes.
A guy with an eye patch who's calling the shots.
A helpful assistant who's last name is Potts.

A girl who takes powers through the touch of her skin.
A guy who guides arrows with a mohawk like fin.
A blue furry guy who's agile and smart.
A doctor of magic and the arcane art.

A girl with the power to modify luck,
A bullet proof man whose as strong as a truck.
A guy who throws cards, that go off with a crack,
A feathery alien that doesn't go quack.

A shapeshifting girl who can be anyone,
A demon who's there and then he is gone.
A telepath merman who also flies,
A guy who likes clobbering all the bad guys.

Holidays

New Year Poem

It's that time of year, when we all drink too much
And we do stupid stuff, examples are such:

You're watching the news just sat on your bed,
You decide to go out and paint the town red.

You drink all night long, but lose count after ten,
You make out with some girls, but find out they were men.

So you wash out your mouth with fowl tasting liquor,
It smells just like bleach, only this one is thicker.

You find out that the glass is filled with sink cleaner,
You have enemies out there, but you know friends are meaner.

So you spend a few minutes with your head down the pan,
But there is good news, drink more beer you can.

Oh boy you feel great, all happy and dizzy.
You've drank so much beer, your urine is fizzy.

You take all your clothes of and dance on the bar,
You try to drive home and you wreck your new car.

Spend the night in a ditch at the side of a road,
Now you feel sick, you just gotta unload.

So you're lying face down in your puddle of hurl
It can't get any worse, but here comes a girl.

You wish you had drunk not quite so much booze,
You should have stayed home and watched all the news.

Xmas Poem

I've been reading the list of who's naughty and nice,
Your names on the list, but it's on the list twice.

It's in with the naughty between Zoey and Bill,
It's in with the nice, but it's there in Pencil.

Someone's been changing Santa's long list,
They better watch out coz Santa is pissed.

He's filling his bag, with prezzies and coal,
But your gift is missing, perhaps it's been stole.

Oh boy Santa's angry, of that I've no doubt,
No wait, I have got it, I've figured it out.

He's located your gift; it was here all along,
But it's not very pleasant; it's got quite a pong.

Its brown and its sloppy, it's a problem to wrap,
What you're getting this year is Reindeer crap.

Xmas 2019

The true meaning of Christmas is different for us all,
The awkward conversation, that annual family call.

The hanging of the Christmas tree and the fights that come with that,
Wrapping covered boxes half opened by the cat.

Dusty decorations that have seen better days,
Tiny little reindeer, pulling tiny little sleighs.

Numerous bowls of candy placed for guests to munch,
But if I go to eat them, "stop, that will spoil your lunch"

The face that we all make when we're opening our gift,
The thrill we try to show, while we hide the kinda miffed.

The endless line of food we eat, might as well be at a trough,
The weight that we all gain that's never coming off.

Tinsel in the cat litter box making tethered strings of poop,
Be careful in the holidays, it can be tough to scoop.

The movies we all watch, we've seen so often we are scarred,
Like Willy Wonka's Chocolate Factory, Sound of Music, or Die Hard.

Poems for Work

Invite to Work Thanksgiving Lunch

(for Enfora Thanksgiving Lunch 2008)

Please attend our Thanksgiving Lunch
Bring a dish we all can munch.

The party will be 21st of November
That's the Friday before, so it's easy to remember

In the employee lounge is where it will be,
So bring your dish for all to see.

Your dish can be hot, your dish can be cold.
Your dish can be mild, your dish can be bold.

Side dish, appetizer, or dessert will be great
Just be there by 12:00 and don't be late.

But please don't bring green eggs and ham.
No one likes them, Sam I am.

A Poem for Debbie

To Debbie Thompson

When you're feeling down and kinda blue,
And you're moping around, don't know what to do,
Think of us at the red white and blue,
At Tektronix

When you've too much to do that you can't think straight,
And you've too many tasks, too much on your plate,
Think of me your Training Manager Mate,
At Tektronix

When you're not very happy and you feel home sick,
Life gets you down and gives you a kick,
Think of us being beat by a stick,
At Tektronix

When you feel like moving, your feet start to itch,
You're not very happy; you're life's in a ditch,
Just think you could still be working for Rich
At Tektronix

When you're sitting upset and you're missing back home,
The Reunion arena, the Cowboys Stadium dome,
Think of me your Training Room Gnome
At Tektronix

Au Revoir Blake

Oh Blake Howell, it's been a freaking blast,
The six years that I've known you have gone by real fast.

I hope your future's awesome, the best that it can be,
And that you'll come to your senses, go from Apple to PC.

I wish you all the best in your life that's yet to come,
Just think of us and smile if you're ever feeling glum.

Adios, Sayōnara, bye-bye, so long, adieu,
We'll see you on the flip side, so for now it's toodle-oo.

A Poem for A Work Colleague's New Baby Hezekiah

Congratulations it's a boy, you've known that for some time,
He came a little early, so I've got to rush my rhyme.

Congrats on the arrival of your little boy,
I'm sure that Hezekiah will bring you lots of joy.

We all saw the picture, a swaddled little chap.
He looks like a burrito in his blanket wrap.

At only six pounds seven he started life quite small,
I bet when he is grown up he could be six feet tall.

Little Hezekiah, congratulations on your birth,
We are glad you're here, welcome to this Earth.

A Scavenger Hunt[6]

A scavenger hunt in digital form,
I send out the email and prepare for the swarm.

But barely a peep I hear from the crowd,
Maybe my email got stuck in the cloud.

I wait a bit longer, but I'm still hearing crickets,
Then all of a sudden in come two tickets.

When I get a submission, I send the next task,
A simple email is all that I ask.

Then after the email, what mission is next?
A ticket for help through an SMS text.

Just one more task before you can rest.
A review of our service to round out the quest.

For those that joined in we thank you a ton,
For those that completed here's what you've won.

---

[6] Sent out to the company to help roll out a new help ticket system.

Karate Poems

Ode to Sensei

Sensei is a teacher, the one who came before,
But to me he's something else, to me he's something more.

He's a shepherd as he guides us, on this journey we call life,
He helps us through our troubled times, our conflict and our strife.

He's a minister to lead our spirits, to make us more complete,
Our mind, our body and our soul, from our heads down to our feet.

He's a bodyguard that protects us, from thugs and criminal types,
He teaches us to defend ourselves, from fists and knives and pipes.

He's a PE coach who shows us all, to dig in and find the strength,
To run the race to the finish line, no matter what the length.

He's a therapist that keeps us sane, he makes us look inside,
Sometimes it's good, sometimes it's bad, that's just our Jeckal and Hyde.

He's a counselor, who brings us up, when we're feeling somewhat down,
He's a father figure to all the Kyu's, from white belt up to brown.

The Unwavering Spirit - (6th Annual Gasshuku - 2003).

We frolicked through the fields, we played with Chi shi weights,
We ran in great big circles, we ran in figure eights.

Up and down and round and round, they're messing with my head,
I know just how the white belts feel, they wish that they were dead.

We did pushups by the thousands, sit ups by the ton,
Go to lunch, don't dawdle, the day is not yet done.

We were pushed out to the limit, then pushed a little more,
We were punched, kicked and elbowed, and thrown down to the floor.

This year the eggs were sloppy, but at least the bacon's real,
The wind was cold, the sun was bright, and now I've started to peel.

But the poem is not just about, the sixth annual Gasshuku,
It's also about friends, and the world around us too.

So I'd like to pledge allegiance, to my Senseis and my Kai,
To promise all my karate ka, the hardest I will try.

Before this school my life was good, but now my life is great,
I owe it all to Isshinryu, TIKK is first rate.

I'm proud to have some teachers, as sincere as you lot are,
I think of you as family, you're as close as ma and pa.

This karate journey that I take, is like a mighty quest,
But if today my life was stopped, I know I've tried my best.

Give all that you have got, in everything you do,
If today you can only do one, tomorrow try for two.

It doesn't seem quite right, when we feel sorry for our self,
Our muscles may be aching, but at least we've got our health.

Our economy is not too good, our nation is at war,
Soldiers are out there dying, yet we complain that we are sore.

I fight to build my character, while others fight to keep us free,
I can't fight for this country, but I can be the best me I can be.

Be the best you, you can be!

Conceive, Achieve, Believe - (7th Annual Gasshuku 2004)

This was the seventh Gasshuku
Fourth for me, for some brand new.

But even for the returning few
There were many firsts at this Gasshuku

The first time for a tornado fright
The first time for a judged skit night

The first time for a junior black belt
The first time tiger balm was not smelt

The first time for a female teen
But not the first time for a drag queen

The first time Sensei promotes to Ni Kyu
The first time we counted all the way through

The first time we put the banner up
The first time I went without my cup

The first time so many came to the shiai
Just imagine the volume if we all did a kiai

First time for many, last time for none
I can't wait till next year's fun

In order to achieve the ideas you make
You first must conceive the path you will take

In order to achieve the difficult feat
You must also believe the problems you'll beat

A Poem for the 8th Annual Gasshuku 2005

April 15th, before sun-up
We arrive at the Gasshuku, with an empty cup.

The pushup ladder, now that's always fun,
With a boom-shak-a-lak-a during the run.

Were given some insight to Rule number 9,
And the reason we stand where we do in our line.

First we learn walking, then learn to crawl,
Then we learn running but that is not all.

We may learn to crawl before learning to walk,
But we also should listen before starting to talk.

From unloading the trucks to the final kumpai
I look back at the weekend, and how it flew by.

Each year it gets quicker, or so it appears,
Filled with good feelings and maybe some tears.

We sang and we danced and told some jokes,
We toasted marshmallows and drank some cokes.

We had two big bad wolfs, and six little piggies,
Guys multitasking smoking some ciggies.

Willy and Waylon, pickin their strings,
Rotating palms blowing whistler things.

Some funny things walking into a bar,
A bunch of drunk students going home in a car.

But it wasn't all laughs and joking around,
We spent much of the time with our face in the ground.

We got sweaty and dirty, we got battered and bruised,
We got shown so much stuff, we got really confused.

Our cup is now full, full of many new things,
A new look at life, is what the Gasshuku brings.

This was the Gasshuku of 2005,
We were all born, to be alive.

Karate Vacation

Some go on a skiing trip, some go on a yacht
Some go once a year, some go quite a lot

They vacation in Hawaii, they vacation in New York
They go on a safari, all to get away from work

But our annual getaway, is different from the rest
We spend our weekend trying to turn ourselves into the best

For three days long we all compete, to be the best that we can be
Not to beat the other kais, but for me to beat just me

We push ourselves out to the limit, and we do it with a yell
We go somewhere only we can go, we vacation in our personal hell

Karate Tournament Poem

Karate Ka, you're on deck
Am I nervous, am I heck

I kneel and watch as they perform
Their chosen Kata, their chosen form

I wasn't nervous while waiting in line
But I'm up next, it's my turn to shine

I bow and enter ring number four
Approach the judges, bow once more,

Announce my form and bow again
Step back, begin and start the pain

A moment later and I am done
But I feel good and I feel strong

I stand and wait for the judges score
I bow again and leave the floor

To announce the winners, the judges stand,
A judge calls my name, I shake his hand

I'd won a trophy, I was a star
But don't strut yet, it's time to spar

Duck and weave, kick and punch
My stomach's growling, I forgot to eat lunch.

Two opponents I just beat
I'm up for first, but I find defeat.

So I place second, that's not too bad
It's all about the fun, and that's what I had

So shout out loud, don't be a mouse
Isshinryu is in the house.

Role Playing Related

Tales of Valornia

Once upon a time, in a land far away
Lived a Half Elven pirate on a quest from the Fae

Her Journeys path crossed with a wannabe knight
And an elf from the mountains, as black as midnight

They fought assassins and mages, goblins and orcs
They capture a human, who pirate then porks

They uncover a plot filled with danger and strife
At the end of this journey, will be great loss of life

An army of humans an army of beasts
An army of heathens starting to feast

Stealth must be used, so must some cunning
But in the end, you can't beat some running

How do you kill the un-killable foe
Do you chop off its head? the answer is no

Find horny pony, gather some hair
Find bad guy's wrists, and tie strands right there.

Once body falls and the spirit is free
It remains in this plane, for you freely to see

Cleave it in two with a cold iron blade
The quest is now over, a great game you have played.

A Poem I used as a DM

To find the sands of time you must
Grind the dragon's bones to dust

To the powder add some dew
Gathered when the day is new

Add two drops of virgin's tears
A hair or two from a black cat's ears

Use widdershins to stir the paste
Slow and steady, use no haste

Pour into a vial of glass
Now you wait for a week to pass

The Extra Poems - Political Stuff

The following are the poems I wrote during April in 2020 and 2021 but didn't send. They were either not appropriate to send to work colleagues or I felt they were incomplete during the month of April.

Politics aside, I cannot hold my tongue,
We really need some fresh blood, we need our leader young.

Concerned about the planet and its people too,
A leader with compassion, not a lying bag of poo.

If money's all they think of, and greed is all they feel,
While the poor can't pay their health bills without missing their next meal.

I'm ashamed to be a human if this is what it means,
Let's wipe out all the cronies and replace them with the teens.

Our economy's in trouble, i'm really not surprised,
The government's to blame cos it's really polarized,

You have the right wing retards with their businesses and wealth.
They don't care one iota for the people and their health.

But then there's the loony lefties, whose brains are kinda runny,
The lefties are too generous with other people's money.

You know there are some numbers beyond the number two,
It's not required to have two teams, we could have quite a few.

There is a middle ground you know, it's called a compromise,
The other countries do it, but I guess that they are wise.

The US is quite backwards, but they think that they're so strong,
They should take their head out of their ass and see they got it wrong.

There was a giant cheeto, with tiny little hands,
He ruled a nation full of lemmings, spread across the land.

His specialty was lying, he did it really well,
Was it true or was it lies, the lemmings couldn't tell.

They gathered at his rallies, they wore his baseball cap,
They fell for what he spouted even if he spouted crap.

When will the lemmings wakeup, when will the rose they sniff,
Or will they all just follow that cheeto off the cliff?

I don't care if you are left wing, I don't care if you are right,
The reason we are in this mess, this crisis, and this plight.

Is the government's response time, or maybe lack of it,
The president's down playing was just a load of shit.

There's one man whose responsible, he's sitting at the top
He is the one in charge, he's where the buck should stop.

He shows no sign of remorse, he won't accept the blame,
To him it's someone else's fault, to him it's one big game.

He claims he's doing great, but the rules he hasn't read,
A bigger number isn't better, it means that more are dead.

He thinks his power's absolute, he's really quite a dick,
Has there ever been a president that has been quite so thick?

Has there ever been a president that's been quite so dumbwitted?
He does deserve to pay for the crime that he's committed,

I say that we should lynch him, hang him from the gallows,
And stream that sucker live, we can watch while toasting mallows.

We have a common problem, with a liar at the top,
When he gets behind that podium the lies just will not stop.

When Potus gets a question he really doesn't like,
He runs off to his mommy, or passes it to Mike.

He calls the news teams fake, he calls their question mean,
He's a fat little shit head, who really is obscene.

He wants people to praise him, he wants his ratings great,
And when things don't go quite his way, he really gets irate.

But I don't blame this Potus, It's not his fault one bit,
It's the ones that voted for him, that are so full of shit.

Other Poems With No Titles

I get up in the morning and do my abutions,
First task of the day? make caffeine solutions.

I try to be quiet, don't wake up the females,
I fire up my computer and check on my emails.

With my inbox all empty, I am ready to start,
I write a tech class to make people smart.

Log into the servers to see if they're running,
Write my plan for the day, and make that plan cunning.

Put on some music to motivate me,
Then back to the kitchen for another coffee.

Check the help tickets, who needs my assistance?
Can it be resolved from a safe six foot distance?

Oh I wish us humans had McAfee or Avast,
All the millions with a virus, would recover real fast.

Oh I wish us humans had Kaspersky or Symantec,
We'd have a lot more healthy, we'd have a lot less frantic.

Oh I wish us humans had some Malwarebytes,
It might stop the panicking, give us a lot less frights.

Oh I wish us humans had some Sophos or some Norton,
Then we'd all be happy, cos isolation time would shorten.

Oh I wish us humans had Windows Defender,
This virus would be beaten, this virus would surrender.

I wish an anti-virus were made for the human race,
We'd beat this covid-19 and that would be quite ace.

To the species in the future, long after we're forgotten,
When our buildings have all crumbled and our corpses have all rotten.

We are sorry for the state of the planet we left you,
We really kinda trashed it, we trashed it through and through.

To the species in the future, please be smarter than we are,
Do not spoil this great planet, and leave a planetary scar.

Treat all nature with compassion, and your neighbors all with grace,
Or you'll end up greedy gluttons, just like the human race.

Who would have thought just this time last year,
We'd be sitting inside cowering in fear.

Cleaning our hands till they are red raw.
Wearing our masks when we go to the store.

Talking to family through computer cam,
Filling sandwiches with three year old spam.

Listening to children as they cry and winge,
Watching the TV while we netflix binge.

It's 4 am and time to eat, oh what am I to munch?
I could have leftover pizza, nah I will save that for lunch.

It's 5 am it's now snack time, back into the kitchin,
I could have leftover pizza, it really is quite bitchin'

It's 6 am time for food, I've only eaten twice,
I could have leftover pizza, I'd only eat one slice.

It's 7 am I'm still hungry, what am I to eat?
I could have leftover pizza, with lots of cheese and meat.

It's 8 am and my mouth is bored, on what am I to snack?
The wife comes in and says to me now put that pizza back.

The dinosaurs were wiped out by a meteor it's said
Now there are none left, they're all completely dead.

Each species time is limited, and humans are the same,
But ours won't be a meteor, we'll have ourselves to blame.

It might be a deadly virus, it might be a third world war,
It might be some friendly aliens knocking at our door.

It moves through the stars at a hell of a rate,
Rushing past planets, as if it were late.

Past Pluto and Neptune, and Uranus it zings,
Flashing past Saturn just missing it's rings.

Then almost got caught by Jupiter's mass,
Just one more planet now it must pass.

It speeds on past Mars, for all it is worth,
It's on it's last leg of it's journey to Earth.

It sees the blue marble just off in the distance,
It's heading this way to wipe out our existence.

It impacts the ground like 10 billion nukes,
Turning most lifeforms right into spooks.

(Alternative April 23rd 2020)

Here is the forecast for day twenty three,
Another day in with just you and me.

I'm not sure what day of the week we are on,
How many are left, how many are gone.

I've started a tally with marks on the wall,
I've painted a face on my big basketball.

I prepared a bonfire to signal for help
I sent out some messages on twitter and yelp

I spelt the word help out of rocks in my yard
I've started to wear the wife's leotard

I joined a few calls and forgot to press mute,
I dance round the house in my birthday suit.

(Alternative April 10th 2020)

Today it is Good Friday, but as far as I can see,
The world is in a crisis, it don't look good to me.

Some have lost their parents, and some have lost their spouse.
We can't even see our sick friends while we're locked inside our house.

One hundred thousand deaths, across the world so far,
It will change the world we know, it's going to leave a scar.

So is this the big finale for which the Christians wait?
When all of them will make a dash for the pearly gate.

One point six million humans around the world are sick,
So pray a little harder, that might just do the trick.

Notes for Poem April 21st 2021

Nelix, Phlox, Odo, or Spock,	Star Trek
Andre', Cactus or maybe The Rock	Wrestlers
Aragon, Gimli, Gollum, or Merry,	Lord of the Rings
Blue Bell, Breyers, or Ben and Jerry.	Ice Cream
Eugene, Patrick, Squidward, or Gary,	Spongebob Squarepants
Eobard, Hunter, Wally, or Barry.	The Flash
Trillion, Zaphod, Marvin, or Ford,	Hitchhiker's Guide to the Galaxy
Duke, Prince, Baron, or Lord.	Titles
Jimmy, Carl, Goddard, or Sheen	Jimmy Neutron
Lucifer, Balthazar, or Constantine.	John Constantine
Lister, Rimmer, Kryton, or Cat	Red Dwarf
Leo, Ralph, or Splinter the rat.	Teenage Mutant Ninja Turtles
Sirius, Draco, Dobby, or Newt,	Harry Potter
Yondu, Drax, Rocket, or Groot.	Guardians of the Galaxy
Lando, Yoda, Chewie or Han,	Star Wars
Kal-el, Clark or just Superman	Superman
Neo, Morpheus, Cypher, or Tank	Matrix
Dale, Jeff, Bobby, or Hank	King of the Hill
Cohen, Mort, Rincewind, or Death,	Discworld Novels
Romeo, Yorick, or maybe Macbeth.	Shakespeare

Made in United States
Orlando, FL
04 July 2022